Walking
GOWER

100 Miles – 25 Rambles

Based on the original work
by Albert White

Prepared 1998
by the Publication Sub-committee of West Glamorgan Ramblers,
Peter Beck John Davis Peter Thomas Albert White & Kate Wynds,
Sid Craven and Marian Davies.

This third edition builds on previous editions . We remain grateful to Mr. George Edwards of the
South Wales Evening Post for technical assistance and to Mr. Tony Lewis for editorial support
during the production of the first and second editions

ISBN 0-9518780-1-8

Typesetting, Printing and Design by
D W Jones (Colourprint) Port Talbot
Cover picture :
At Fall Bay, Rhossili - looking towards Thurba Head by Gordon R. Howe

Acknowledgements

For this edition we are indebted to Mr John D. Varley of Llanishen, Cardiff, and also to Morganite Electrical Carbon Limited, for generous assistance. Thanks are also due to the Gower Society, Julia Berney, for permission to use illustrations, Glamorgan Wildlife Trust and finally, to all those Group members who have given of their time and support.

In this third edition of the Guide, minor revisions of the text have been made to reflect improvements to the footpaths carried out since publication of earlier editions.

Maps based on the 1992 Ordnance Survey 1:25,000 map with permission of the Controller of Her Majesty's Stationery Office.   © Copyright

Walking gives pleasure to so many people and Morganite Electrical Carbon Limited ⊃⊂⊃⊂ is pleased to support this excellent guide to Gower which has proved so popular over the years.

Further Reading

A Portrait of Gower, W V Thomas, 1976; A Guide to Gower, The Gower Society; The Natural History of Gower, M E Gillham, 1983; The Gower Coast, G Edmunds, 1985; Historic Gower, P R Davis, 1986 and 1997; Yesterday's Gower, J M Thomas, 1982.

The Ramblers' Association

LOCAL groups of the Ramblers' Association help in practical ways to maintain rights of way, clearing overgrown paths and stiles, waymarking and monitoring generally. If you encounter obstructions, accidental or deliberate, when out walking in Gower, please report them to the local authority's footpaths officer. You are entitled to remove sufficient of an obstruction to enable you to pass, but if this is not practicable you may have to find a convenient way round. Take care not to damage property or crops and be sure to leave gates as you find them. If you would like to know more about The Ramblers' Association, please write to The Ramblers in Wales, Tŷ'r Cerddwyr, High Street, Gresford, Wrexham LL12 8PT, telephone 01978 855148, fax 01978 854445 or e mail : cerddwyr@compuserve.com

Foreword

It gives me great pleasure to contribute the Foreword to this excellent guide for those looking to explore the Gower Peninsula on foot, and I thank the West Glamorgan Group of the Ramblers' Association for their kind invitation.

The City and County of Swansea is committed to encouraging sustainable activities on Gower, as part of the overall tourism portfolio. Gower was the first part of the UK to be designated as an 'Area of Outstanding Natural Beauty' and I feel sure that this selection of walks will enable both experienced ramblers and those of us who are less committed walkers to appreciate the delights that Gower can offer.

I would urge everyone who visits the countryside to respect the environment to help ensure that it can be equally enjoyed by generations to come.

Councillor B Owen, JP
Chairman
Economic Development Sub Committee

"There's a wind on the heath, brother; if I could only feel that I would gladly live for ever"

George Borrow, from LAVENGRO, Chapter XXV

Introduction

THE idea of walking around Gower was first suggested to me by Dave Allen, (WGR Footpath Officer at the time) and I began to investigate possible routes in the early 1980s. Rather than just walk around the coast, I decided to make a series of circular walks going out along the coast and returning via an inland route, thus enabling most of the features of Gower to be included in one walk or another.

There is a very wide range of scenery, wildlife and historical interest in Gower. Most of the 1100 flowering plants found in Glamorgan are present in Gower, while about 150 species of bird can be seen at some time of the year.

The archaeologist can find much of interest too, ranging from prehistoric Paviland Cave and its famous bones of the Red Lady, to Arthur's Stone burial chamber and impressive Iron Age forts. Later, Celtic saints founded many churches and the Normans have left stone castles, churches and villages.

Rural life continued until recent times with very little industrial development, the most notable exception being the Mumbles Railway, which had the distinction of being the first passenger railway in the world. Many of these features are described in greater detail later. The Gower area has had its share of famous people, too. Wynford Vaughan Thomas, author and broadcaster, and Dylan Thomas the poet (1914-1953) were both born in Swansea and have written extensively about Gower. Vernon Watkins the poet (1907-1967) lived at Pennard, Daniel Jones the musician was born in Swansea and Ceri Richards the artist was born in Dunvant. Much earlier was Isaac Hamon, of Bishopston, who described the language, geology, natural history, people and life of Gower in the 17th Century. Thomas Bowdler (1754-1825), the expurgator of Shakespeare, lived at Oystermouth and is buried there, while Beau Nash (1674-1761) was born in Swansea and later made Bath the fashionable centre it is now. We should also not forget Edgar Evans (1870-1912) who was born at Rhossili and perished tragically with Scott at the South Pole.

Finally, the charm of Gower is well summed up by J C Woods, who wrote the following for a British Association meeting in Swansea in 1883:-

'Linger with me this olden land to spy:
A land of sleepy hollows, hemmed with woods
And hill-slopes dense with deep-roof'd solitudes;
Of wind-racked moors o'er which the curlews cry,
And the red waves of rolling gorse-fires fly:
Of capes and scaurs, sea hewn in stormiest moods,
And roaring caves, that nurse the kestrel broods,
Where once old-world carnivora crawled to die.

A land whereon the breath of Arthur's praise
Floats like a mist; around whose rock bound coast
Lie Philip's galleons rooted fast in sand,
Hovers in storm-time many a drown'ed ghost.

A shore for song, a land of yesterdays:
Linger with me about this haunted land."

May you enjoy your walking in Gower!

ALBERT WHITE

The Walks

THE walks in this guide are all circular and have been planned to provide a number of variations. The 10 basic walks make up 100 miles and 7 of them can be split by means of short cuts, enabling a choice from 25 walks to be made, from 5 to 13 miles long.

The routes mostly follow rights of way, while others are on permissive paths, country lanes, or on open access land. In the south, the Heritage Coast is featured.

All the routes were checked on the ground by WGR in 1998, but changes of detail may occur subsequently. Care needs to be taken on cliff walks and warning notices heeded, but none involves risk provided common sense is used. Walks 7 and 9 are not recommended in poor visibility, nor after heavy rain.

All distances are approximate. Do not underestimate the walks as there is some quite rugged terrain. Allow yourself 2 miles per hour. In addition to sensible walking gear, secateurs and a walking stick can be very useful at times.

Gower is largely grazed by cattle and sheep. Dogs need to be kept under strict control.

Background information appears throughout the route descriptions, highlighted by the use of italics. In addition, longer, separate features can be found on Prehistory, Limestone, Churches, Castles, the Mumbles Railway, and Mumbles Pier, Islands and Lighthouse.

The symbol ● is used to indicate where a short cut rejoins the main route.

The following abbreviations and terms are used:

Cadw - Welsh Historical Monuments	Burrows - Sand Dunes
CCW - Countryside Council for Wales	Cwm - Valley
GR - Grid Reference	Hayes - Enclosed field
GWT - Glamorgan Wildlife Trust	Lake - Stream
NNR - National Nature Reserve	Pill - Stream
NT - National Trust	Pound - Enclosure for stray animals
WGR - West Glamorgan Ramblers	Slade - Coastal Valley
	Tor - Rocky Peak

The Ordnance Survey Explorer 164 1:25,000 map which covers Gower shows rights of way and field boundaries but needs to be used with discretion.

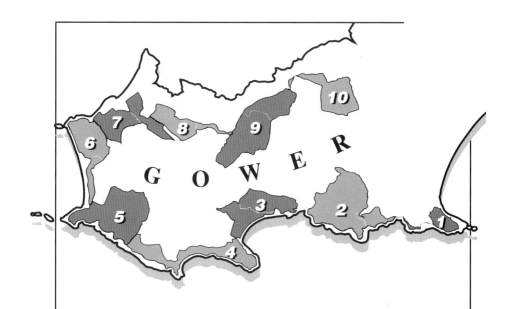

Oystermouth - Caswell　　　1

THIS short walk introduces some of the popular bays and cliff scenery of the South Gower coast. There are many points of interest, including: Oystermouth Church and Norman Castle; Oystermouth itself (once a centre for oyster fishing) with its old cottages on the steep hillside; Mumbles pier; and the Bishop's Wood nature reserve and countryside centre at Caswell. By combining some or all of these features a full day's outing can be planned.

Distance : 7 miles (11.2km)

The walk starts from the sea front in Oystermouth opposite the White Rose public house. Oystermouth is well served by buses and has several car parks.

Walking away from Swansea, go along the sea front on the promenade, which used to be the track of the Mumbles Railway. This way doubles as a cycle path so remember to keep to the pedestrian lane. In a little over ½ mile (0.8km) the path runs close to the road and opposite the George Inn.

On the right of the inn, a flight of steps (Dickslade) goes steeply up, past old fishermen's cottages, onto Mumbles Hill, a local nature reserve with fine views over Swansea Bay, Mumbles Pier and, beyond, the lighthouse on the outer head.

Continue in the same direction, with the bay on your left, soon descending towards the main road, with a small headland called the Tutt, with its coastguard station, straight ahead. To the left is Bracelet Bay and, to the right, the smaller Limeslade Bay.

Cross the road and walk along the pavement around Limeslade Bay, then through a gate onto the cliff path which leads in about ½ mile (0.8km) to Rotherslade with the Osborne Hotel just beyond.

After a short flight of steps turn right through a gateway and climb more steps up to the hotel car park. Bear left around the hotel to another flight of steps which rise up, passing an electrical sub-station, to reach the main road on a bend. Turn right and walk up hill on the main road passing traffic lights and take the first left turn after the traffic lights into a lane. Follow the lane to the end and turn left to descend by a flight of steps to rejoin the main road outside the

WALK 1

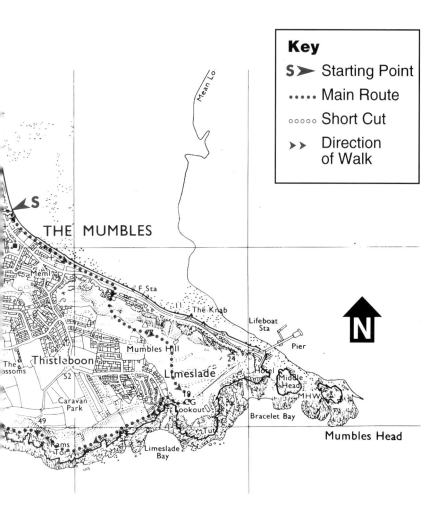

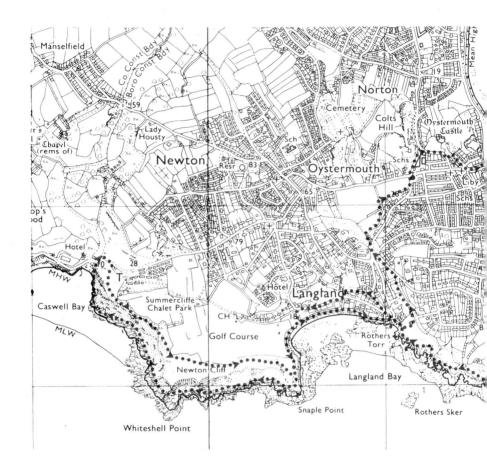

Manselfield

Co. Const Bdy
Boro Const Bdy

59

Norton

Cemetery

Colts
Hill

Oystermouth
Castle

er's
Chapel
(rems of)

Lady
Housty

Sch

Newton

Resr

83

Oystermouth

Schs

Lby

Sch

op's
ood

65

79

Hotel

MHW

0

28

T

Hotel

Langland

Caswell Bay

Summercliffe
Chalet Park

CH

18

Rothers
Torr

B

MLW

Golf Course

Newton Cliff

Langland Bay

Snaple Point

Rothers Sker

Whiteshell Point

1 entrance to the Langland Bay Convalescent Home. Turn right along the road, do not enter the driveway to the Convalescent Home, and after a few yards enter a public park by a gate on the left towards tennis courts. Follow a path to the right keeping the tennis courts on your left until you reach a large car park. Cross along the top side of the car park and out onto a narrow road, turn left down hill between walls to the sea front path.

Turn right on the path and, after reaching the western end of Langland Bay, carry on along the cliffs, around Snaple Point to Whiteshell Point, then on to Caswell Bay (shops, toilets) and the main road, about one mile (1.6km) from Langland.

Turn right along the road for 100 yards and just before a building, the Bishop's Wood countryside centre, go right, through the trees and steeply up an indistinct path to reach a golf course and cliff path, high above the path you have just left.

Keeping to the seaward of the golf course, continue to a small headland overlooking Langland Bay. Here the path swings right, descending to join the metalled cliff path. Turn left and walk along the path above the beach until back at Rotherslade beneath the Osborne Hotel.

Continue forward and in about 100 yards take a narrow path left up the slope passing a seat. When another path is met at the top of the slope, opposite another seat, turn left and follow this level path to steps and a road. Go left and come to a junction of several roads.

Cross over to a bus shelter, turn right and very soon left through a gateway and down steps to Underhill Park recreation ground. Keeping to the right, cross the park, turning right at a children's play area to leave by another gate.

Go left along the road to a cross-road, straight over and along a lane, turn right at a junction and continue along a back street to Oystermouth Castle.

After viewing the castle, continue via Castle Street, turn left along the main shopping street, at the end of which is the White Rose public house and the starting point.

Village Lane, Mumbles

Mumbles Railway

Following the success of the Swansea Canal it was originally intended to extend this to Mumbles to carry limestone from Mumbles and coal from the Clyne Valley. However, the plan was eventually dropped in favour of a tram road and an Act of Parliament was passed on 29th June 1804 authorizing this, a year before the Battle of Trafalgar. The tram road carried only goods initially and commenced at Brewery Bank in Swansea, adjacent to the Swansea Canal, and ran along the sea front to Castle Hill, Oystermouth. It was not until 25th March 1807 that passenger traffic was inaugurated by Benjamin French, "Gentleman of Swansea", one of the original shareholders, using a horse drawn wagon. This made the Mumbles Railway the first passenger railway service in the world. Until 1826 the line prospered, but then a road was made between Swansea and Oystermouth and competition from horse drawn buses led to closure of the passenger service prior to 1830.

However, in 1855 the line was relaid and the passenger service recommenced but it was not until 1877, when steam traction was introduced, that it became really popular, though the fact that both horse and steam power were used by two rival companies on the same line caused many wrangles until 1896, when the horse drawn service ceased. In 1898, the railway was extended to the pier at Mumbles. The line reached its peak of glory in the period before the first world war and carried as many as 40,000 passengers on a bank holiday. In 1929, the line was electrified and continued to prosper until after the second world war. The post war car boom led to its decline and, on 4th January 1960, a train left the Rutland Street terminus for a special ceremonial journey to Southend/Mumbles and back. The last public service was run on the following day.

In spite of the nostalgia nowadays for the passing of the railway not everyone at the time felt so. Richard Ayton in 1813 said: "The passage is only four miles but it is quite sufficient to make one reel from the car at the journey's end in a state of dizziness and confusion of the senses that it is well if he recovers from it in a week". For this pleasure the charge was one shilling. Dylan Thomas reminisced that "we took a tram that shook like an iron jelly down from our neat homes to the gaunt pier", while the poet Walter Savage Landor, who lived in Swansea for a while, referred to "the detestable tram road". Remains of the train that are now to be seen include the front cab of No 7 electric train at the Maritime and Industrial Museum, Swansea, and an electrical sub station at Blackpill.

Mumbles Pier, Islands and Lighthouse

THE pier was opened in 1898 when the Mumbles Railway was extended. The decorative cast ironwork is noteworthy and the structure is 800 feet long. There used to be concerts, choral competitions, fireworks, aquatic displays and sports. One day in the 1930s, 20,000 people visited the pier by land and 3,000 by sea. It was last renovated in 1956. The present lifeboat station is on the pier and can be visited in the summer season. It was completed in 1916 and replaced the previous station near the Knab. 757 people to date have been saved by the two lifeboat stations, with the loss of 18 lifeboatmen. A previous lifeboat, the "William Gammon", is now moored at the Swansea Maritime and Industrial Museum.

It is possible the name Mumbles derives from the appearance of the two white limestone islands, looking like breasts, or in Latin "Mammae" or Danish "Marmles". The islands can be visited at low tide for about 3 hours by going along an old wartime causeway. There has been a lighthouse on the outer island since 1793. This originally had a coal fired beacon and, later, oil and then gas fired burners. Now a solar powered 100 watt quartz iodine electric light is used. There are 2 100W 12 volt lamps giving off a total of 13,700 Candela (Candle Power). Three Abraham Aces were keepers for almost 75 years.

There is a large sea cave at the end of the outer island which is the most extensive in Gower. It is called Bob's Cave and the pirate John Avery was hanged near here in 1731. Traditionally, the pirate Bob kept his plunder in the cave.

Common Rock-rose

Caswell - Threecliff Bay 2

A LONGER walk along cliffs and through wooded valleys. A short cut is possible from Pwlldu Bay up Bishopston Valley, if preferred.

Distance : 12 miles (19.0km)

The walk begins from Caswell Bay car park and bus stop. Turn right out of the car park and walk up the road for a short way. Opposite Caswell Bay Court turn left down a narrow footpath, by the entrance to Bay House, and cross the beach to a concrete wall and along to a flight of steps. At the top turn left, following the cliff path around to the right, and then on to the tiny inlet of *Brandy Cove*.

Further along the cliff path the prominent storm beach of Pwlldu comes into view. The cliff path eventually reaches a cross path above the beach. Turn right on a stone bedded path, uphill to join a rough lane and then left down to the back of the bay. Cross a stream by a footbridge and turn right to a stile.

(From here a short cut may be taken by going up the Bishopston Valley (NT) for about ¼ mile (1.2km), keeping the stream on your right, to a footbridge where the main route is rejoined at ●).

Do not go through the stile but go sharply left up a rocky path through woodland. At the top leave the trees and bear left along a track to houses. Left of these go through a gate and follow the path with a tree plantation on the left, to cross a field to a stile. Now follow the field boundary, descending to steps and a stile. Cross the stile and continue to the bottom of the steps and on to meet a grassy track. Turn right, uphill to rejoin the field boundary. (Note the banks of High Pennard promontory fort on the left).

Keeping the field boundary on your right, cross the open cliff land to a metalled road at Hunts Farm. Turn left and keep on the road to reach Southgate and the large NT car park (shops and toilets). Nearby, in the cliffs, are Minchin Hole and Bacon Hole caves, famous for their prehistoric remains.

Keep to the left hand side of the car park and follow the single track road with houses on the right. Just before the road ends bear left onto a bridleway which continues along the cliff top to a headland above Pobbles Beach and the

WALK 2

© Crown Copyright Reserved

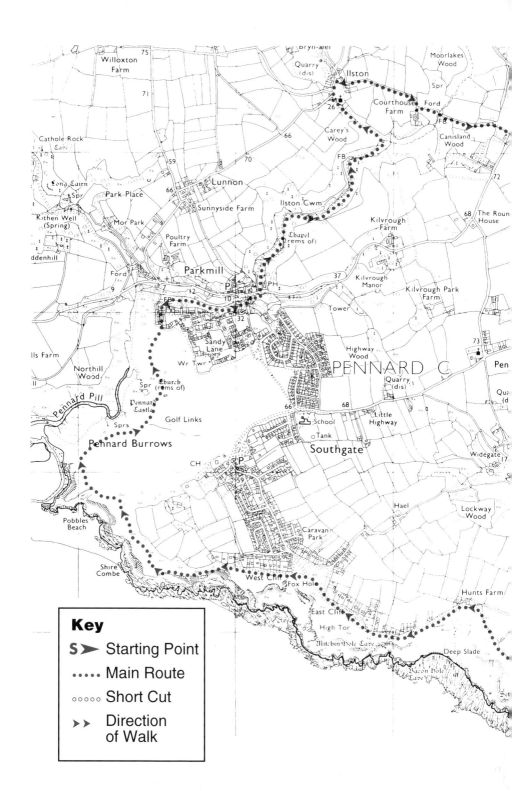

Key

S ➤ Starting Point

•••• Main Route

ᴏᴏᴏᴏᴏ Short Cut

➤➤ Direction of Walk

spectacular Threecliff Bay.

Drop down from the cliff path to the shallow valley on the right. Take the path towards the beach then bear right to a slatted path with steps, which skirts a golf course. Follow this path, keeping to the higher ground above the valley, with Pennard Pill winding below and Pennard Castle ahead.

From here the path bears left, still skirting the golf course, and, after passing some chalets on the right, descends into a small copse. At the bottom go right and drop down to the stream by a footbridge. Do not cross this bridge. (In Parkmill, the original mill complex has been restored and is open to the public).

Carry on through woodland, keeping roughly parallel to the stream, along a narrow path for about ⅓ mile (0.5km). Just after a stone, marking the boundary of the old parishes of Ilston and Pennard, the path emerges onto the metalled lane from Parkmill to Sandy Lane. Cross the lane to a footbridge over the stream and turn right along the A4118 towards the Gower Inn. Just before the inn a footpath goes left through iron gates and alongside the stream again into Ilston Cwm, where there is another old boundary stone set in the wall above the stream.

The way passes the site of the first Baptist chapel in Wales and continues over seven bridges, passing Ilston Cwm cave on the opposite bank just before reaching Ilston Church. Keep left through the churchyard, leaving it to cross the stream again and walk right, along the road through the village.

Take the first right and go through a gate, usually open, along the drive to the Old Rectory. Just before the house turn sharply left alongside a wall then right to a rough sunken lane. The lane ascends gently then narrows to a stile at the end. The track resumes, going right and sharply left past the entrance to Courthouse farm, to descend to a stream which is crossed by 2 wooden bridges. Go through the gate ahead and follow the track as it climbs gently, and, after a stile, emerges onto the main road. Take the road opposite, signposted Kittle, and on to pass Kittle Hill dairy farm, then Stonegate egg farm after a double bend.

Just after the farm entrance go through a metal kissing gate and follow the path alongside poultry houses, running parallel to the road. Cross a stile and continue along the hedge to another stile where the road is rejoined for a short distance to Kittle at a T- junction, with the Beaufort Arms public house on the right. (St. Teilo's Church, Bishopston, is situated nearby at the head of Bishopston Valley, and can be reached by a steep lane left of the road junction.)

Cross the main road and opposite the Beaufort Arms turn left by a small green (NT) and follow the track around to the right as far as a farm (Great Kittle). Take the narrow path slightly left which swings left steeply down to the valley bottom, passing a small but deep daw pit (Gulver Pit) on the right.

Turn right and continue along the dry rocky stream bed, passing Guzzle Hole on the right (the underground stream can be heard here) and Longash old lead mine on the left. Shortly, the stream resurfaces and is followed for about ½ mile (0.75km) to a metal footbridge on the left. (Ignore the wooden bridge).

● Cross the bridge bearing left along the main footpath, and within a short distance a path on the right leads uphill passing a set of wooden steps. Take this path (there are more wooden steps) up the valley side to the top. (Just before the top, the overgrown banks and ditch of Hanging Cliff Iron Age promontory fort can be discerned to the right of the path). At the top follow the path straight ahead for a short distance to a seat with fine views of the valley and Pwlldu Bay.

Return the same way to the top of the climb and turn right on the main path, following it to a gate. Go through the gate, continuing on a lane which steadily improves before joining a metalled lane. Turn left on the lane and continue to pass a right turn and then a small parade of shops. After the shops turn right down Brandy Cove Road, at the end of which is a kissing gate with Hareslade Farm on the right. Go straight ahead and, immediately before a gate and stile, turn left up steps to another stile. (There are spoil heaps of an old lead mine around here and a small pit and adit on the left.)

Follow the path uphill and turn right at a T-junction. After a stile a metalled road is reached on a bend. Go right, down the road, to return to Caswell Bay and car park in a little under ½ mile (0.7km).

Brandy Cove

THIS secluded little cove was a centre for smuggling in the last century, not only of brandy but also of gin, tea and tobacco. The smuggler became almost a folk hero and in this area it was the Arthurs of Great Highway and Little Highway Farms (on the road between Pennard Church and Southgate) who were the most famous. In 1804, Customs men discovered nearly 3,000 gallons of spirits in secret cellars on these farms, which had probably been landed at either Brandy Cove or Pwlldu Bay and taken up lanes on horseback. One old lane from Pwlldu is still called Smugglers Lane.

Pennard Castle from Parkmill

Penmaen - Oxwich 3

A WALK of contrasts: from sand dunes to a lofty ridge; a nature reserve to a fine mansion and romantic castle. A short cut is given through Nicholaston Woods, to rejoin the main route near Perriswood

Distance : 9 miles (14.4km)

The start of the walk is at Penmaen Church where there is a bus stop and some parking space north of the church, just off the road on the right hand side (GR 532888).

From the church, cross the main road and go along the lane opposite, after about 200 yards turn right. At the end of the lane, by an emergency phone, turn right downhill, with a fence on your right, passing the gate and stile into Stonesfield. Continue to the bottom and another emergency phone.

At the bottom bear right and cross a small stream, bearing right again to climb steeply up a sandy path through bracken and scrub to the top of the cliffs at Penmaen Burrows.

Turn right and continue ahead to find the remains of Penmaen old church on the right of the path. The walls still stand to a height of four feet but are in a depression and can be difficult to find. The megalithic tomb of Pen-y-crug is about 200 yards south of the church and is well preserved. Continuing south towards the cliff edge, Penmaen Old Castle's high bank and ditch are ahead, commanding the view of Threecliff Bay.

Bear right around the cliff path to the prominent headland of Great Tor, which separates Threecliff Bay from Oxwich Bay. Continue along the cliff path for about 200 yards to meet another path from the right, near an old lime kiln. Passing the kiln, follow the cliff path to a stile at the top of the high cliff.

Stay on this top path to a second stile on the right. Opposite, descend on a sandy track to a slatted path at the bottom.

(For a shorter walk , do not descend here but continue on the upper path until it descends through trees and becomes sandy. At the bottom go left for a short

18

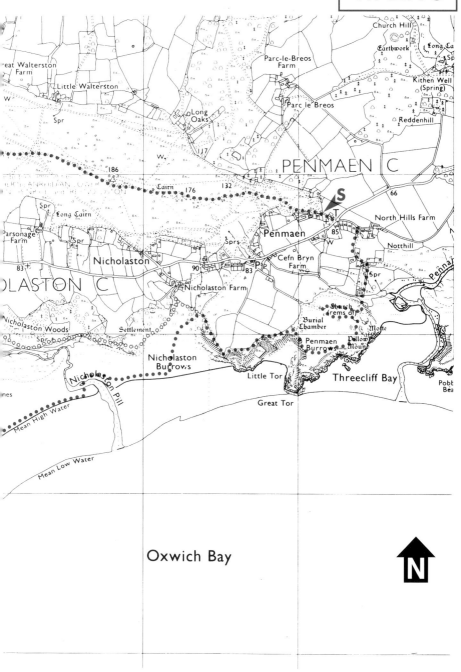

WALK 3

© Crown Copyright Reserved

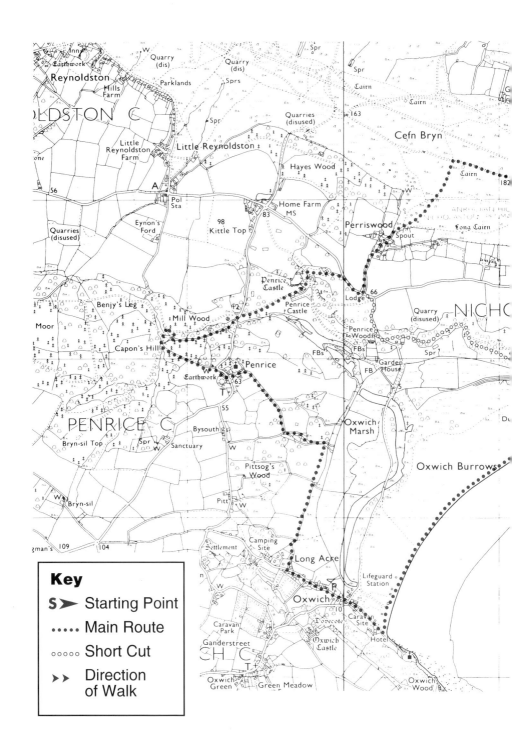

Key

S ➤ Starting Point

•••• Main Route

ooooo Short Cut

➤➤ Direction of Walk

3 distance, then right into woodland to reach a broad path and turn left on this path. Continue just inside the woodland until a small, more open, stand of oaks is reached. This area is carpeted with primroses in spring. Carry on along the wooded path, ignoring paths to dunes, until it rises to pass along the open cliff face, with a succession of viewpoints across the top of woodland and over Oxwich Bay, before dropping quite sharply to meet a broader track at right angles. Turn right and follow the track which winds through Nicholaston Woods to a road. Go right, up to the main road by The Towers at the entrance to Penrice Castle. Turn left for a short distance to the first turning right for Perriswood.●)

Turn left for a short distance through the dunes to the beach. Turn right along the beach and when you come to a stream, Nicholaston Pill, go inland for a short distance to cross by a wooden bridge, then carry on along the sands of Oxwich bay for a little over one mile (1.7km) to reach the Oxwich Bay Hotel.

Leave the beach and turn right onto the road (public toilets) and walk ahead to a crossroads. Continue straight on passing several pretty, old cottages, some thatched, one of which is called 'The Nook'. A plaque records that John Wesley lodged and preached here in the 18th Century.

Just past "Driftwood" on the left, go right over a stile along a narrow path to another stile leading to fields. Keeping to the right hand side of the fields, go straight on to a stile into woodland. Turn left on a path which keeps to the left hand edge of the wood, before bearing right to a stile.

Go half left across the field to join the hedge and follow this, over a stile and along a track up to Penrice Church. Note, on the way up, the lovely view back of lake, woods and cliff towards Pwlldu Head and the Glamorgan coast beyond.

Cross the small Penrice village green and turn right along the road, going steeply downhill for a short distance. At a sharp right hand bend go straight ahead on a footpath through woodland. A few yards in from the road the old Penrice well can be seen beside the path, right.

Soon the path descends to join a forestry road where, turning right, a pond is reached on the right, an old mill pond. Turn right here on another track and, at the end of the pond, take a footpath on the right which follows the course of a leat down to a ruined mill with, nearby, curious quartered circular ponds, old fish or stew ponds.

3

Cross the road to the large ornamental gates into the Penrice Estate. To the right is a stone stile which is crossed to walk up the metalled drive through the estate and between the house and castle, following the yellow waymarks. At a junction, turn left, past a red-brick stableblock, then right, off the drive, continuing to follow the waymarks up to the main road. (It should be noted that the estate is private, and that the castle is unsafe and cannot be visited.)

Turn right for a short distance and turn left up a narrow lane to Perriswood ● a small hamlet with a tiny green. Go half right across the green, along a short stony track and through a gate onto the common of Cefn Bryn. From here the path to the top of Cefn Bryn is not very obvious but the power line is a good guide, that is, slightly right from the gate.

On the very top of the ridge an old rough track is joined and followed to the right. But before doing this, a pause to rest will afford the chance to appreciate the extensive views, from the Somerset coast on one side to the Black Mountains and Brecon Beacons on the other.

The ridgeway is followed down to Penmaen, past the trig. point, marking the second highest point in Gower, and the rocky outcrop known as the Beacon, from its use as a beacon probably from the 15th Century. The track ends by a large and prominent building, Glan-y-mor, and a little further on is the car park and Penmaen Church.

Penrice Village

THIS peaceful little village was once the market town of Gower. On the green is a stone with octagonal socket that once held the village cross, lost in the 18th Century. The stone later became the 'crying stone', from its use by auctioneers at fairs and for the making of announcements. In the churchyard, left of the porch, is a 'murder stone'. The inscription reads.' "To the memory of Mary, wife of James Kavanagh of Penmaen, who was murdered by ....the 3rd of October 1829, aged 75 years." Such stones were erected about this period with the object of encouraging witnesses or attracting the murderer to the scene of the crime where his conscience might be struck, leading to a confession. However, as far as is known, the culprit was never found.

The Church of St. Andrew, Penrice

21

Oxwich - Foxhole Slade 4

This is the longest and perhaps most rewarding of all the walks. It can be done in two parts if wished, using Port Eynon as the point of return. This option is described below.

Distance: 13 miles (20.8 km)

The walk begins from the large car park in Oxwich. The village has a regular bus service.

Turn left out of the car park entrance and left again at the crossroads. Follow the road to the church of St. Illtyd in its sylvan setting. The tiny chancel is reputedly the original Celtic cell. Continue past the church on a path which goes right and up a long flight of steps. Just before the top turn left and follow the main path through woodland, which is part of the NNR, to Oxwich Point, reached soon after emerging from the trees.

Now walk along the low cliffs towards Horton, the next village on the coast, a distance of 2½ miles (4.0 km). On the way, the higher cliffs are a conspicuous feature on the right, relics of a time when sea levels were much higher.

Approaching Horton, the sandy beach of Port Eynon Bay is reached and soon the path leaves the open cliff to go between hedges for a short distance to a private parking area, then as a surfaced road, passing Sea Beach Nursing Home.

At a green, fork left towards a mast marking the inshore lifeboat house, after which turn left to the beach along a slatted path. Go along the beach for ½ mile (0.8 km) until a large obvious gap appears at Port Eynon (shops, toilets).(Here, a short cut can be taken by going inland along the main street for a short distance to the church of St. Cattwg and lifeboatmen's memorial, where the main route is rejoined at ●)

Continue along the beach to the second building, the old lifeboat house, now a youth hostel. Ahead is a ruined building, the Salt House, but our way goes right, beside the youth hostel, between hedges, and meets another path at right angles.

4 Turn left and after 100 yards turn right onto a stony path which winds uphill to the headland, passing over debris from old limestone quarries, to reach a large granite monolith, erected as a memorial to two founder members of the Gower Society. It is through the Society that so much of Gower has been saved for us to enjoy today.

From the memorial continue along the cliffs for about 250 yards, then fork left down to another path. Nearby is the intriguing walled-in cleft of Culver Hole. Turn right and walk around the small rocky bay ahead, Overton Mere. On the far side continue around the head until the path forks, then bear right uphill to a rough road.

Turn left to go between stone walled fields to a stile leading out onto the open clifftop again. There is a plaque here marking Longhole Cave Cliff Nature Reserve (GWT).

The magnificent South Gower Coast now beckons, almost six miles (9.6 km) of the finest cliff walking, part on this walk, the rest on Walk 5. Virtually one large nature reserve, it is managed jointly by CCW, NT and GWT, and is famous for its wild flowers and birds.

The cliff path is followed, close by the field boundaries most of the way to Foxhole Slade, a narrow rocky valley with a stone wall running along the bottom. The path drops to the floor of the valley to a stile, right, in the angle of the walls.

Take this stile to go inland through fields, keeping the hedge on your left, until a large ditch crosses the path. Do not cross, but go right, alongside the ditch, to a stile, coming out onto a farm road.

Turn right to Paviland Manor Farm and pass between the two barns and out to a gate and path with a fence on the right. Before the next field turn left, with a raised bank now on your right, to a stile. Now go half right across the next field to a stile, then ahead past a trig point on your left, to leave a ruined farm, (Hills) right. Go through a gate ahead and along an enclosed track to a cottage (Little Hills).

Follow the track around to the right and down to the small settlement of Overton, where it meets a road. Turn left along the road, past New House Farm, just after which is a stile, right. Cross the stile and go straight over a field to another stile. From here bear left to the hedge and follow it down to another stile which leads into a caravan park.

4

Join the rough track coming in left and walk ahead through the park and out onto the road in the village of Port Eynon. Turn left up the road to the churchyard and lifeboatmen's memorial.

● Go straight on, with the church on your left, and take the second road on the right. Pass through a swing gate then along a path which soon joins a small road. Turn right and, at a T junction, cross to a stile slightly to the right.

Follow the steep path uphill, curving left and right to keep to the crest of the hill, and with field hedges on your left. Where the path divides, keep right and drop down to a stone stile at the head of a small valley.

Cross the stile and immediately go left up a narrow path to a minor road. Walk right, along the road, with good views of Port Eynon Bay, to reach Bank Farm. Go into the main entrance, pass through the farm, keeping the buildings on your left, and down a short slope to come out onto the road in Horton, on a sharp bend.

Go straight ahead, keeping to the top of the village and, when the road goes left, turn right through the entrance to The Beeches farm. Bear left up a slope and, soon after passing the farmhouse, leave the lane by the second gate on the right (waymarked) into fields.

Cross half right to a projecting corner, then follow the left hand hedge to the end of the long, narrow field. Cross a stone stile and the wooden rail fence to go straight on to Western Slade Farm with its prominent silo tower.

Go through a gate and the farmyard, then along a track to a minor road at the top of the hamlet of Slade. Continue ahead, past Eastern Slade Farm, to Oxwich Green. Here, the chapel has been converted to make an attractive residence.

Soon after the green, the road, called Ganderstreet, swings left and descends to a junction, just before which is a stone stile on the right. Go over the stile, into a field and make straight for Oxwich Castle, whose impressive gatehouse faces you.

4 Leaving the field by a gate, turn right then left to go between the castle and the farm. Once through the farmyard bear left towards a boundary fence. Follow this down a rough bank, with no clear path at first, to a stile which leads to a rough track and soon, the road.

Turn right downhill to the crossroads in Oxwich and go straight over to return to the car park.

Lifeboat Tragedy

A LIFEBOAT station was established at Port Eynon in 1884, following the loss of 25 lives in shipwrecks a year earlier. However, tragedy befell the lifeboat itself in 1916 when there was a call to the SS Dunvegan, in danger off Pennard during a severe westerly gale, and three crew were lost. The marble memorial erected in the churchyard overlooks the road. After this disaster the lifeboat station was closed and is now a youth hostel.

Culver Hole

THE inside of the wall has many holes, suggesting its probable use as a dovecote, similar to the pigeon houses at Penrice and Oxwich Castles (culver = dove, pigeon). Traditionally, Culver Hole is associated with the Salt House as a smugglers' hideout and there is the inevitable story of an underground secret passage between the two, "whereof no man was tolde the mouthe thereof."

The Salt House

THE well preserved remains are those of a salt factory which closed in about 1657. Sea water was partly evaporated in shallow chambers, then boiled in large lead or iron pans until salt crystallised out. The salt was used mainly for curing meat and fish. There is an interpretive panel on the site.

Prehistory

ARCHAEOLOGY in Gower goes back to the Palaeolithic or Old Stone Age which ended around the time of the last Ice Age, 10,000 years ago. There were only a few scattered families at that time, living by hunting and on berries and plants. Remains of that period are few and mainly found in caves which offered shelter and an area at the front for cooking and surveillance. Many such caves were along the south coast of Gower, overlooking the Bristol Channel, where the sea was much lower than at present. The most famous of these caves is Paviland which has been found to contain palaeolithic animal remains such as the woolly rhinoceros and reindeer, as well as thousands of flint implements, but is most famous for a find of part of a human skeleton that came to be known as the "Red Lady of Paviland".

The first recorded exploration of the cave was in 1822 by the Davies brothers, Donald, a surgeon at Reynoldston, and John, curate of Oxwich and father of the Rev J D Davies (who wrote the "History of West Gower"). Their finds included the tusk of an elephant and this led to a further excavation in 1823 by Miss Jane Talbot of Penrice, Lewis Weston Dillwyn of Swansea, and the Rev William Buckland, Professor of Geology at Oxford University. These excavators found the bones of the left side of a human skeleton stained red with ferruginous earth and at the same level as the palaeolithic animal bones. Some of these finds are in the Royal Institution of South Wales, Swansea, but the human bones are still at Oxford. At that time it was generally accepted that old animal remains were from before the Flood (Noah's Flood in Genesis) but that man was not present in Britain until after the Flood. Archbishop Usher had, in fact, calculated from the Bible that man was created in only 4004 BC, so it was difficult to reconcile all these facts and finds. Buckland, being a good Christian, concluded the human skeleton was a much later burial and, though he at first thought it was that of a male, the presence of ivory rods and rings persuaded him it must be female, hence the Red Lady. Later work showed the skeleton was that of a young man of around 16,500 BC and the animal bones were left by hunters or were the remains of animal occupants of the cave. These findings helped to lead to the acceptance of the idea that man had evolved from other animals, as shown by Darwin in his "Origin of Species", published in 1859. Other caves such as Cathole in Green Cwm, Parkmill, and Longhole, near Overton, have similar features but no other significant human remains.

The next age was the Neolithic or New Stone Age in which agriculture began to develop in a warmer climate. The major remains from this period are megalithic burial chambers built of massive stone slabs, the most spectacular of which is Arthur's Stone on top of Cefn Bryn. It consists of a massive capstone supported on three of nine uprights and is a double chambered tomb, at least 4,000 years old. The capstone, originally estimated to weigh 33-35 tons, is now fractured, probably due to frost action. It does not appear to be local Old Red Sandstone conglomerate (though it is similar) and it has been suggested it is Millstone Grit conglomerate brought from further north by glacier movement during Ice Ages. Even if this were so, some limited shifting of the stone would probably have been needed. Whatever the source, however, the Welsh Historical Triads considered it one of the three mighty achievements of the Isle of Britain. Not surprisingly, there are many legends associated with Arthur's Stone. One tells that the capstone was a pebble from King Arthur's shoe, flung away when he was on his way to the Battle of Camlan. Another is that when the cock crows (or on midsummer's eve) the stone goes to the Burry River to drink. Other legends say the capstone was split off by King Arthur with Excalibur, or that St David struck it off to prove it was not a sacred stone. Other megalithic monuments include Sweyne's Howes, on the eastern slope of Rhossili Down, and Giant's Grave (Parc le Breos) near Parkmill.

By around 2000 BC, the use of copper and bronze spread to the British Isles by the Beaker Folk, emigrating from Europe. These people left burial cairns and mounds often with pottery, daggers and cremated remains. Good examples are Great Carn, a large stone cairn near Arthur's Stone, and Pen-y-Crug at Cillibion. Many stone circles date from this period, as also many standing stones such as Samson's Jack. The Bronze Age lasted until about 500 BC when the Iron Age was ushered in by further immigrants from Europe. Competition for space led to warfare between groups and this age is characterized by defensive earthworks, some very large. The largest of these on Gower is Cilifor, covering 7-8 acres and with three concentric earth ramparts. Another very large site is The Bulwark on Llanmadoc Hill, with elaborate multiwall defences, probably built over a long period. The exact purpose of The Bulwark is uncertain and it may have been a large family farmstead primarily for cattle keeping and segregation, with secondary use for defensive purposes in time of war or against raiders. There are also many small promontory forts along the cliff tops of South Gower. Bacon Hole was occupied by man in this period, though animal remains here date back to the Palaeolithic. The Iron Age merged into Roman Britain in 50-100 AD and the beginnings of recorded history.

Arthur's Stone

Pilton Green - Rhossili   5

MORE splendid cliff scenery and an ancient roadway. If it is wished to end the walk in Rhossili, a bus can be taken back to Pilton Green.

Distance: 9 miles (14.4 km)

The start of the walk is at Pilton Green (NT) where parking is possible just off, but clear of, the track to Pilton Green Farm (GR 446871). Buses pass here.

Cross the road slightly left to a stile and path leading to Paviland Cave. Go alongside the hedge through several fields for ¾ mile (1.2 km) to the head of the narrow, rocky valley of Foxhole Slade.

Cross the stile to another stile in the right hand wall and go up the short, sharp scramble onto the cliff top. Keeping the field boundaries on your right, cross the open, grassy area to a stile midway in the wall ahead.

From here bear right up the path, through gorse, soon to join the wall again and meet a crossing point in the corner. Go over and take either of the two paths ahead, veering away from the field wall, towards the sea and another crossing point in a wall ahead.

This wall bisects a small but well preserved promontory fort on the Knave, and is a good vantage point for the magnificent cliffs along to the Worms Head.

Ignore a stile into a field, but keep to the field boundary until it turns inland, and carry straight on across open ground to the next deep valley. Go right, alongside this to its head and then descend the rough path to Rams Grove, a wild, rocky valley.

Climb up the other side, bear left and follow the path again with field walls on your right. Continue, keeping to the wall, with the 200 foot high headland of Thurba looming ahead. This was the first NT property in Gower.

When the wall turns sharp right, go straight ahead (there are small wooden signposts set in the ground here) towards the large valley of Mewslade. Descend into the valley, aiming slightly right for the prominent knob of rock at the bottom.

5

Pass to the left of the rock to a stile in the wall and go straight ahead up a steep slope, turning left at the top alongside a wall to come out onto the open cliff top. Carry on along the wall on a clearly defined grassy path.

When the wall goes sharply right, bear slightly right (along the low bank of Lewes Castle promontory fort) then along the field wall again to Fall Bay, going around a rocky point and down to a grassed-over lime kiln.

Stay on the upper level around the bay, with its flat ledges of rock, towards Tears Point on the far side. Follow the path when it veers left from the wall and head for the projecting field corner, right of Tears Point. At the corner go along the wall, following it around to the right, uphill.

At the top of the slope the Worms Head is dramatically revealed. Continue by the side of the wall, which is the boundary of the Vile, a medieval field system extending from Rhossili village to the cliffs and still in use today.

The wall soon turns inland and is followed all the way to the village. But, before doing so, it is worth visiting the Gower Coast Reserves Centre housed in the small stone building on the headland, the former coastguard lookout. Worms Head can also be visited when the tide is right but probably should be a separate excursion - it takes longer than you might think!

Walking towards Rhossili, the three mile long beach, backed by Rhossili Down and terminating in the islet of Burry Holms, is well seen from these 200 foot high cliffs. Soon after passing the banks of yet another promontory fort, Old Castle, the village is reached (shops, toilets).

The first buildings are coastguard houses, where there is a NT shop and visitor centre. Continue along the village street towards Rhossili Church and, when a bus shelter is reached, bear left and left again along a path around the churchyard.

When the road is met again, turn left down a cart track to a kissing gate at the end giving access to Rhossili Down (NT). Through the gate, bear right past an old stone building (described in Walk 6) and climb the steep slope with steps, keeping right on the clear path.

Do not go to the top but turn right to follow the highest field boundary, fenced at first, then walled. Go straight on where the wall ends, past a white house, to a small covered reservoir, just beyond which is a track.

Turn right on the track for a few yards then leave it, left, and walk alongside a stone field wall down to a rough road by a house and bungalow. Bear left along the road which leads straight to a gate and stile. From here go right along a track to another gate with a high stile in the hedge.

Go over the stile and follow the hedge to cross a small stream by the ruins of Kingshall. Take the stile left of the derelict house, note the old pigsties on the left, and walk through two fields, the first with the hedge on your right, the second with the hedge on your left. In the corner bear left through a small rough patch to a green lane between hedges, Kingshall Lane.

This old Gower road, which has 'escaped' modernisation, still shows traces of its construction and, when it emerges into the open, its line is clearly visible going half left as a slightly raised causeway. After a gateway in a stone wall it continues between hedges again to Old Henllys Farm, once a manor house, seat of the Mansels, an old Gower family.

Immediately past the house, and before a pond, turn right through a gap in the outbuildings, going straight across a field to a stile. Enter a tiny copse over a small stream, going through to a stile. Cross the field bearing slightly left to another stile.

Cross the stile and follow the hedge around, left, to another stile in the corner. Go over the stile, passing through a gap in the hedge, then left and right again around the field to a stile. Now carry straight on with the hedge on your right, down to a gate and another abandoned farm at Newton.

Walk between the deserted buildings and uphill to the end of the field to another gate around a right hand corner, by a water tank. Turn left to go along a stony track to pass a sheep pen and around to the right to a stile and gate by a pond.

Turn left, continuing on the track to go around the barns of Pilton Green Farm, leaving by the gate on your left to return to Pilton Green.

Yellow Whitlow-grass

Worms Head

KNOWN locally as the Worm (the name comes from an old word for dragon) this mile long promontory is accessible for several hours at low tide. The causeway opening times are posted at the coastguard station in Rhossili and published in the Evening Post each day. Two interesting features are the Devil's Bridge, between the Middle and Outer Heads, and the Blow Hole on the Outer Head, where a small fissure near the path, which is connected to a sea cave, produces strange sounds that vary from a low moan to thunderous rumbling and booming that can be heard far away, depending on the tide and weather.

Sweyne's Howes

THESE are two megalithic burial chambers, originally covered by mounds of stones, dating from the Neolithic Age, over 4,000 years ago. They have both been mutilated and robbed in the past and perhaps their main interest to us today is in the name. Sweyne was the legendary founder of Swansea around 1,000 AD: Sweyne's ey, or island, there once having been an islet at the mouth of the River Tawe, being the origin of the name Swansea. At one time, before modern archaeology, it was usual to attribute such antiquities to the Danes!

Rhossili - Llangennith   6

THIS Walk is dominated by the superb Rhossili Bay and Worms Head, seen at first from the low cliffs, then from the breathtaking heights of Rhossili Down. A short cut is described which retains both of these features.

Distance: 9 miles (14.4 km)

THE route starts at Rhossili Church. There is a large car park at the far end of the village and buses terminate here.

Just past the church, on the road back to Swansea, bear left along a track to a gate with a kissing gate alongside. Go through and bear left past a small stone building, the former rocket house. It was from here that a line would be fired across a shipwreck, thus enabling a breeches buoy to be attached to haul the crew ashore.

A path goes along the foot of the down, past the old rectory, and from here it is a little over one mile (1.8 km) to Hillend caravan park. At the far end of the park, a gate on the left leads to a metalled road by the entrance to the caravan park.

Turn right on the road for a few yards, looking carefully for a gap in the privet hedge on the left. By peering through this gap, two old cannons may be seen in the grounds of Hillend House. These came from the "Dollar Ship" wrecked in Rhossili Bay in the 17th Century.

(For a shorter walk, go back through the gate and, turning left, follow the path that goes NE to the boundary between the open down and fields. Continue alongside the wall, past a house and a farm, until the wall ends and a track comes in from the left. Now turn right.●)

Return on the road to enter Hillend caravan park, keeping to the right hand road to the dunes. At the end of the road, by an emergency telephone and before the car park, turn right along a rough track behind the dunes, continuing on a path to a small river, Diles Lake.

Turn left and follow the river through the dunes onto the sands of Rhossili Bay. Turn right and walk along the beach for about one mile (1.4 km) towards Burry Holms, a tidal islet which may be visited at low tide.

6 Take the path in the NE corner of the bay and climb to the top of the cliffs to the left. Continue along the cliff path through the dunes with Bluepool Bay opening up on the left. This takes its name from a natural rock pool in the far corner of the bay. In the dunes to the right of the path are the remains of a stone walled Iron Age settlement, usually hidden by the sand.

Stay on the cliff path until reaching a boardwalk by a waymark post. Follow this boardwalk all the way down to Broughton Bay Caravan Park. The last small headland, Twlc Point, is on your left as you descend.

When the road through the park is reached turn left and, just after passing the buildings of Broughton Farm, take the stile on the right. Go straight ahead, keeping the hedge on your left, up to a field gate. From here go left through another gate to come out onto a track. This is Cockstreet, the name recalling the gaming and cock fighting once carried on here. Along this street the first horse bus to Swansea left in 1896.

Turn right along the track, which soon becomes metalled, towards Llangennith. Just past a road junction with "Bus Stop" painted on the road, take a left turn along a narrow, stony lane. When the main road is met at a T-junction, turn left into Llangennith, a typical Norman Gower village, the houses, Church of St Cenydd and old tavern grouped around a small green. Note St Cenydd's well, now covered over but still providing a constant supply of clear water.

Leaving the church on your left, go down a narrow lane to Coety Green, a deserted settlement with remains of cottages and a corn mill around the green. Cross the stream over a wooden bridge and go left of the farm entrance along a stony lane to come out onto the open moor. In a few yards the stone wall on your right turns to the right.

● Now carry on along a path through the bracken up onto Rhossili Down straight ahead. When the first rocky crest is met go left and then right across a hollow to the top of the Down proper. Follow the clear path left all along the top of the Down, passing the remains of a wartime radar station.

Soon a green track is met and followed. To the left, the Sweyne's Howes can be seen some way off the track but, by now, the views seaward are irresistible. In about ½ mile (0.8 km) the highest point of the Down (and of Gower) is passed and soon the descent to Rhossili begins, past the rocket house again and back to the church.

Tankeylake Moor - Cheriton 7

THIS rather less frequented corner of Gower, with its unspoilt villages and sweeping views of estuary and marsh, makes for pleasantly varied walking. A short cut is described from Llanmadoc, rejoining the main route at The Bulwark.

Distance: 9 miles (14.4 km)

The starting point is Tankeylake Moor (GR 435916) just before the village of Llangennith. Parking is possible just off the road and buses pass here.

From the junction of a farm track and the main road, take the green track going left, alongside the hedgerow, and follow this around to the left to an overhead power line. Leaving the hedge, continue straight ahead, climbing slightly, then descending to a metalled road, Cockstreet.

Carry on along the road, which becomes unmetalled, go through a gate and continue until the track swings right. Here, go left over a stile and straight ahead to another stile to walk downhill, with the fence on your right, towards the sea.

After three further stiles, turn left on a sandy track past Broughton Farm and then right by a collection of old ships' anchors to come to the beach, Broughton Bay. Turn right along the beach to a stream, cross over and follow it inland to a kissing gate and emergency phone. Turn left, walking behind the dunes along a sandy track.

When the track goes right, keep straight on and walk along the left hand side of a large caravan site, Whiteford Bay Leisure Park. Keep close to the park boundary to its end, where there is a stile and metalled lane.

Go over the stile and turn right along the lane up to the road by the park entrance. Turn left and walk along the road to Llanmadoc Church and the old rectory opposite with its great overhanging roof. Parson Davies was rector here (and of Cheriton, where he is buried) for over 50 years, from 1860 until his death in 1911, and he rebuilt the rectory after a visit to Switzerland. He is best known today for his fascinating 'History of West Gower'.

7

(For a shorter walk, continue past the church and small green on the right to the village post office and general store. At the telephone kiosk take the right hand fork and soon reach another small green. Here fork right then left along a narrow path to emerge onto the open hillside. Keep to the right hand path past a house and climb steeply up until a path comes in sharply on the right. Just past here take the right hand fork and continue uphill on a pleasant green path. On reaching a rough track, turn right ●)

From the church turn left down a lane to the hamlet of Cwm Ivy, and at the end bear right and go through a gate beside a NT sign for Cwm Ivy. At the bottom go right through a gate, and along a broad track through conifers towards Whiteford NNR.

(Visitors are welcome to use the marked paths on the reserve and from here to Whiteford Point is 2 miles (3.2 km). It is an important site for breeding and wintering birds, and there is a small non breeding colony of eider duck which can often be seen near the old cast iron lighthouse.)

Before a warning sign turn right, go through a kissing gate and walk along the sea wall. This dates from the 17th Century and was built to reclaim the marsh from the sea for grazing. It is maintained by the NT whose purchase of Whiteford was the first of Enterprise Neptune, the campaign to protect our coastline. In season, the saltmarsh is full of colour, with pink thrift, sea lavender, silvery sea wormwood and marsh mallow, in succession.

At the end of the sea wall, cross a stile and go straight on with woodland on your right. After passing two cottages (note the ancient beehive pigsty between them) continue past an old stone boathouse to a gate and stile. There was once a harbour here but all is now silted up.

A short steep ascent brings you to a metalled lane between houses. Turn left to the main road and left again to a fork in the village of Cheriton. Bear left past the Britannia Inn and soon reach the church.

Opposite the church, turn right over a stone stile into a field and go straight ahead, keeping left of the hedge, to a stile into a copse. Continue with the fence on your right to another stile, then a short length of boardwalk, and emerge into fields. Keep to the right hand boundary, soon with the *Burry Pill* below, crossing two stiles before turning right over the next stile into woodland.

Now cross the stream on a low stone bridge and follow the rough track uphill and around to the left, when it becomes a level, grassy path with the steep slope of Ryer's Down on the right. On the left is a house with millstones set in the wall (Western Mill) and the path continues as a stony track. When this rises slightly and bears right, turn sharply right onto a broad path which leads up onto Ryer's Down.

Climb up the path keeping the field boundary on your left until, near the top, the hedge swings left, there go straight on along a clear path. Ahead, in the distance, is Llanmadoc Hill and you should aim for its right hand end where the earthworks of The Bulwark can be discerned. As you descend, make for a waymark post near a culvert beside a rough track and before a small copse, cross over the track and follow the waymark through the copse, alongside a low bank, to a stile in the fence on the far side.

Go over into a field, with a hedge on your left. In a few yards cross another stile and then right alongside the hedge to a stile and a road. Walk right, along the road and take the first left, a rough track which goes up onto Llanmadoc Hill.

The track passes the ruin of a school (closed in 1935) and further on, on the left, the former farm of Stormy Castle. Turn left here, off the track and alongside the wall, climbing steeply past the house, just after which the track is met again and followed on up the hill.

● Where the track turns left, go straight on through the obvious gap in the earthworks of The Bulwark, then, keeping to the middle of the enclosure, continue until a wide, green track swings half left along a ditch, then right again and straight on along the top of the hill, aiming for a trig point and cairn at the far end.

About midway between The Bulwark and the trig point, however, the way goes half left and then descends gently, gradually curving around to the left and down onto Tankeylake Moor, and back to your starting point.

Burry Pill

PILL is the local word for a stream or small river, and Burry Pill is the largest of the streams in Gower. In spite of its modest size, however, there were once seven corn mills operating on it and there are records of these 'grist' mills as far back as the early 13th Century. The main source of the pill is near the village of Burry, from where it meanders northwards to reach the sea between Whiteford Point and Landimore Marsh. Here it is known as the Burry Inlet or Estuary but, due to dredging it is no longer apparent. Hard though it is to imagine today, John Wesley crossed the estuary on horseback from Whiteford Lighthouse to Pembrey in 1764.

Sea lavender

Landimore - Llanrhidian 8

Another walk in this quiet corner of the peninsula; fairly easy going, but a short cut can be taken if wished, described below.

Distance: 8 miles (12.8 km)

The route starts at Landimore, where there is a small car park at the end of the village, by the marsh (GR 464936). Buses to Landimore are infrequent, so it would be more convenient to start and finish at Llanrhidian church and village green, if using public transport.

From the car park walk back up the road, passing a large lime kiln, with Bovehill (NT) on the right. The slight remains of Bovehill Castle are high above the road on private land. At the NT sign it is possible to walk steeply up to view the castle from the perimeter hedge of a small wood. From the castle, drop down half left through a gap between houses to rejoin the road. Landimore was once a busy place with a small port, three public houses, shops and a school.

A little further along the road turn left over a stile into fields. Go straight ahead to a waymark post (on your left) turning right to pass through a gate. Go half left across two further fields, crossing two stiles, then half left again to aim for a field corner between a fence and woodland. Cross the stile into a long narrow field with the woodland on your right. Continue ahead and, as Weobley Castle (Cadw) comes into view, follow the wood as it bears right to a stile in the corner. Continue ahead across the next field to a stile, where a rough road crosses the path.

(For a short cut, turn right here uphill to the main road. Turn left along the road for a short distance to a metalled road on your right, which leads to Windmill Farm ●).

Continue straight ahead along the waymarked route with the open marsh on the left, bearing right below the castle, through bracken. The path contours along the bottom of the hill and, in about 300 yards, goes through the hedge over a stile into a field.

Turn right along the hedge, then enter woodland, crossing two stiles, and join a rough lane coming down from Leason. Follow this, left, into the open again. On the left is the rising of Leason Pill where a mill once operated. Its ruins and mill pond are still visible.

Cross the stile on the right and follow the well waymarked path which keeps to the right of the fields and the edge of woodland until, in a little over ½ mile (1.0 km), it meets a track just south of Staffal Haegr, another old mill, now producing spring water instead of woollen goods.

Keep straight ahead on this track, which becomes metalled, then follow it around left into Llanrhidian (shop, public houses) with a stream on the right. The road next goes right, over the stream, where there is a view of Nether mill and pond. Go ahead, then right, through the village to the green with the church set back on the right, approached along a path flanked by a pair of stones, erected in the last century although both are much older.

Take the next minor road, right, above the village green (the alternative starting point) up to a T junction, turn right again and continue straight ahead to old quarry workings. A path goes through these uphill towards a field boundary, then bears right to a corner, to continue alongside the left hand hedge. The hillside is a GWT reserve and commands a fine view over the village to the Burry Estuary.

Go through a gate into an enclosed lane, passing a farmhouse on the right. The lane leads through the farm and, just after a metal clad barn on the right, to a stile into a rough field and another stile. Straight ahead, past a house, a stile leads out into fields again.

Follow the left hand hedge downhill to a stile and a lane, crossing the bed of a small stream and up to a stile. Go straight ahead to another stile and, after crossing, turn right with the hedge on your right. Cross a further stile and continue until the hedge bends to the right. Here, go ahead to a stile, cross the next field towards buildings. Do not go over the first stile alongside a gate, but go left for a short distance to a second stile, coming out into a lane. Turn left into the hamlet of Leason.

Continue ahead, passing the house 'Middle Leason' on your right. Ahead down a lane, and just before the farm at the bottom, turn left to follow the track around to the right and a double stile. Go half left to a further stile, crossing fields to cross a stone stile out onto the Oldwalls - Llanmadoc road. Turn right for about 200 yards and then left along a road, initially metalled, to Windmill Farm.

● By the farm, take the left hand gate into a field and follow the hedge on your right. In the second field a large standing stone, Samson's Jack, is in the hedge on your right. Continue along the hedgerow, passing Manselfield Farm on the left, before joining the Oldwalls - Burry Green road.

Turn right along the road past Stembridge Farm and down a steep hill. After a sharp left hand bend cross a stile alongside a gate on your right to pass Stembridge Mill. Once past the buildings keep alongside Burry Pill through fields to a crossing of paths. Just to the left here is a quaint, low, stone bridge.

Still with the pill on your left, continue through the fields, passing the stone lined leat of the long abandoned Stone Mill. After going along a boardwalk and through a copse, the main road is reached opposite Cheriton Church in its beautiful setting.

Turn right up the hill past Glebe Farm, its present day appearance belying its history as the oldest surviving domestic building in Gower. When the road swings right, take the path straight ahead through a gate and along a green lane to a second gate. Continue straight on up to and through North Hill Farm, after which bear left along the hedge to a small gate at the end. To the left is North Hill Tor, haunt of ravens. Go through the gate into woodland and make the short, steep descent to the shoreline.

The way, right, now continues along the foot of the wooded cliffs, with the saltings on the left. High in the cliffs approaching Landimore is Bovehill Pot, Gower's deepest cave, and soon you are back in the car park.

Raven

Standing Stones

THE large standing stones, or meini hirion, of which Samson's Jack is a good example, have for long been a source of fascination. Their exact purpose is not known: sometimes they are associated with burial or ritual functions, while some occur on or near ancient trackways, but there is no evidence of either of these purposes in Gower. They are generally attributed to the Bronze Age. The remarkable thing is their concentration in western Gower: eight still exist in this small area, and the implied presence of others, now lost, from field names, eg Long Stone, Broad Stone, Stone Field, in the same area, suggest a total of 20 or more.

Churches

AFTER the Romans left Britain, around 400 AD. Wales became rather isolated. Missionary holy men, generally called saints, from Gaul and Ireland, and later from Welsh sites, travelled around and at suitable sites built "llan" enclosures. Here they erected wooden crosses and simple huts surrounded by earth embankments. Services would be held here and eventually graves dug for the faithful. Larger sites and monasteries became established and were named after the saint, eg Llanilltyd Fawr was the Llan of St Illtyd. After the Norman Conquest and an increase of population, stone churches were built, often on the old Llan sites. It is these churches, built mainly in the 12th and 13th centuries that are seen today.

Burry Holms and Llangennith were founded by St Cenydd in the 6th Century and traces of a wooden oratory and a walled enclosure were found within the medieval buildings of a small hermitage on Burry Holms. A llan was also established in Llangennith (Llan of St Cenydd) at around the same time and became a 'Bangor' or college of some importance. It was destroyed by the Vikings in 986.

The true origins of St Cenydd are obscure, though he was probably a pupil of St Illtyd at Llanilltyd Fawr (Llantwit Major, South Glamorgan). When he was eighteen he built a simple cell by a spring, probably at Llangennith Green. The Holy site was later neglected, but was restored by St Caradog towards the end of the 11th Century and, when the Normans conquered Gower, a Benedictine priory was established on the same site. The present church was probably built in the 13th century and is the largest in Gower. Within the church, on the west wall of the vestry, is an ornamental slab claimed to have covered St Cenydd's grave, though it is more likely part of a slab cross. A 15th Century manuscript infers that St Cenydd's skull was preserved as a saintly relic which was used to swear oaths upon.

There are very fine examples of wood carving in and around the church by Mr Bill Melling, who lived just opposite the church. The lych gate depicts the legend of St Cenydd, while a casket next to the pulpit shows scenes in the life of the church, such as the Viking sacking in 986 and the Norman building. The church is also the burial place of the Welsh Prince Iestyn ap Gwrgan, mentioned on the David stone at Penmaen Church. There is an interesting mutilated effigy of a knight near the font, traditionally called the Dolly Mare and supposed to be a member of the de la Mare family, who held lands in the area.

Llanrhidian - The name derives from St Rhidian (possibly a Celtic saint trained by St Cenydd or by the wife of St Illtyd) who is considered to have founded a Llan here in the 6th Century on the site of the present church, dedicated to St Illtyd and St Rhidian. This present church is one of the oldest in Gower dating from the 13th Century and it was granted to the Knights Hospitallers of St John in 1167. There is a massive tower with a large masonry block on the SE corner of the parapet called the Parson's Bed. This was used as a fire beacon to give the alarm when enemies were approaching. The church was extensively restored in 1856 and 1900 and contains wood carvings by the Rev J.D. Davies of Llanmadoc - 324 bosses for the ceiling of the nave, all different, and an oak altar. In the porch is a sculptured slab, known as the Leper Stone, dug up near the tower in 1865, thought to be of 9th or 10th. Century date. The carvings show Irish influences and the scene may represent the meeting of St Paul and St Anthony in the desert, a subject common in Irish art of the pre Norman period.

Rhossili - The origin of the village name is uncertain but is probably from Rhos Iley - moor stream The original Celtic village lay at the foot of the Down in the corner of the bay, but was abandoned after it became besanded. The site has been excavated in recent times and there is an account of this in the church. The present building is apparently 13th Century but incorporates a fine Norman doorway, with chevron and dogtooth mouldings, which seems most likely to have come from the old church. It is a typical simple Gower church with saddle-back roof and strong tower, probably used as a place of refuge at times of raiding and warfare. Like many Gower churches it used to belong to the Knights of the Hospital of St John of Jerusalem until the dissolution of such orders by Henry VIII in 1534. On the north wall of the nave is a white marble memorial tablet to Petty Officer Edgar Evans, RN, who died with Captain Scott on his ill-fated journey back from the South Pole.

St. Cenydd's Church, Llangennith

43

This walk, whilst not one of the longest, involves some rough terrain with no clear paths. Note that the marsh road may be flooded at high spring tides. A short cut is described via Llanellan, and if the section over the moor to Arthur's Stone is omitted, it is possible to return to the start by using the Cillibion to Llanrhidian road.

Distance: 9 miles (14.4 km)

The route starts from Malt Hall, the first left turn off the main road through Llanrhidian village. Parking (with consideration towards residents) and bus service.

Continue along Malt Hall, and take the first road turning right, leading down to the village with its green, standing stones and church. Passing the Welcome to Town, right, and the Dolphin, left, both old taverns, keep right at the junction and follow the road out of the village as it winds down to the extensive Llanrhidian Marsh (NT).

Walk along the road, passing the prominent hill of Cilifor Top, to a side road with a cattle grid (note the ramps to enable small creatures to escape!).

(Here a short cut can be taken by going right, along the road through Little Wernhalog to the main road. Turn left for a short distance to a slight rise and gate on the right. From here a path goes uphill through bracken and, when a grassy area is reached, go between the power lines and the ridge ahead along a rough track. When this swings right, look out for a slight path going left up through bracken again onto the top of the ridge. Go straight ahead along the ridge, over a stile and through Llanellan Farm. Continue along the farm road to reach Welsh Moor Farm, just after which turn right on the road over Welsh Moor (NT).●)

Carry on along the marsh road, past the Cocklers' road out onto the marsh at Wernffrwd, to a junction where the road bears left to a bridge over the Moorlais River. Just after the crossing, go right on a rough track which passes the side of Crofty Mill, right, of which little can be seen today. After a kissing gate, follow a surfaced path to the main road.

Cross over to continue on a footpath alongside the river. At a rough track go right, over the river again and, very soon, bear left on a footpath between houses to Llanmorlais village. Turn left along the street, past Llanmorlais Farm, right, a good example of a Gower long house, to reach a small green.

Bear right, up a lane, which becomes a rough track crossing open ground, where there are disused mine workings, now overgrown. Keep on the track uphill to reach a junction. Go straight over and follow the track around to the left and up to a pair of semi detached cottages, where the track ends.

To the right of the cottages a gate leads to a path, through woodland, to a kissing gate and onto a farm track. Turn left to a metalled road, then right, along Bryn Common, to reach a road junction just beyond Bryn Farm. Keep straight on to another, larger common, Welsh Moor (NT), with a track to Welsh Moor Farm, right.

● A few yards further on, strike out across the moor half left (roughly south) towards woodland. There is no distinct footpath at first but, as you near the woods, the way becomes clearer and aims for the right hand corner of the woods. Now a rough track appears and crosses a stream to go through a gate.

The track, called Black Lane, goes along the edge of the woods and between hedges. In a little over ½ mile (1.0 km) a main road is reached at Cillibion. Turn right along the road and fork right at the junction. (Stay on this road for a little over 1 mile (2.0 km) if not going to Arthur's Stone).

In about 200 yards (opposite footpath sign to right) go half left onto the open moor, aiming for the low bracken covered mound of Pen y Crug, a bronze age tumulus. (The left hand line of telegraph poles is good guide). Passing the tumulus on the right, now pick up a reasonably wide grassy track, initially on a bearing of 260 degs. Broad Pool (GWT) is visible to the left, with its sheet of yellow water lilies in late summer.

Now look for Moormills, a large sink hole, making roughly for a farm complex (Stonyford). Some of the water disappearing underground here resurfaces almost a mile away at Llanrhidian.

On the far side of Moormills, continue across the moor, heading towards the ridge of Cefn Bryn ahead, aiming for the low saddle just left of the highest visible point, to the left of which can be discerned Arthur's Stone. The crossing of this moor can be very wet, and deviations from a direct route often become

45

necessary. However a clear path, uphill, is soon reached and at the top it meets a green cross track.

Turn right here and soon reach Arthur's Stone megalithic tomb, a good spot to rest and enjoy the view. There are many other relics of early man on this glorious ridge, but we must move on.

Return to the green lane and take a grassy track directly opposite Arthur's Stone, descending, to aim for the right hand side of a white house with red roof (Freedown).

Go through a gate and into the yard of Freedown. Cross the yard, pass the house and, on reaching the drive, turn right through a waymarked field gate.

Cross the field half left to a stile in the far corner, passing a large overgrown sink hole. Go right, over the stile and along the hedge to the next stile, erected in memory of Bob Cunningham, founder member and first Footpaths Officer of West Glamorgan Ramblers.

In the next field go left along the hedge, then right, to a stone stile deep in the hedge. Cross the stile and go straight ahead to the main road. Turn right for a short distance and take the lane, left, by the school, which soon brings you back to Malt Hall.

Buzzard

Long Houses

IN Europe, long-houses date from the Neolithic Age but the local form is later, probably early Medieval. The human quarters and byre were under one roof, separated by a cross-passage with doors giving direct access to the two sections. In the living area an open hearth backed on to the wall of the cross-passage. By the 16th Century fireplaces, chimneys and upper storeys were added, and the central entrance replaced by separate doorways. Another example of a long-house is Western Slade Farm, passed on walk 4.

Limestone

LIMESTONE is visible in the magnificent cliffs along the South Gower coast, which culminate in the Worm, a long snake of land beyond Rhossili. Especially between Port Eynon and Rhossili, the cliffs show the intense folding and distortion which produced the Cefn Bryn backbone of Gower. These cliffs support a wide range of characteristic flowers, eg, vetches, rockrose, samphire, spring squill, bluebell, bloody cranesbill, thrift, scurvy-grass (a good source of vitamin C at one time) and yellow whitlow-grass, a Gower speciality.

Limestone has been quarried for many years for building, limewash and lime for agricultural use, and is still used for road building. Remains of quarries are all along the coast, especially at Mumbles, Pwlldu (where the unwanted small stone has formed a huge stony beach), Port Eynon and Rhossili. Here, at Kitchen Corner, the ledges used to load boats can still be seen. Over 150 lime kilns have been recorded in Gower, and remains of these are common. Some have been restored and a good example can be seen at Bovehill.

Limestone also underlies much of inland Gower and is responsible for various interesting landscape features, due to the tendency of limestone to dissolve slowly in water. This solution is accentuated in cracks and faults, leading to underground streams and caverns. In the Bishopston Valley the stream begins on impervious shales to the north and disappears underground by Bishopston Church, when it meets the limestone (though in heavy rain it can flow overground.) This underground stream can be heard and seen at Guzzle Hole, near the end of the subterranean section, and surfaces again, or rises, a little further on when it meets more impervious ground. An important rising is at the end of Green Cwm where the flow is utilised by Welsh Water, to be pumped up to a reservoir on top of Cefn Bryn.

Large pits and saucer shaped depressions can be seen where underground caverns have collapsed. The upper part of Bishopston Valley has several such pits, called daw pits (as jackdaws nest there). There are also many depressions in the open moor north of Cefn Bryn, called sink holes. The largest of these is Moormills and several streams flow into this sink and re-appear at various points on the North Gower coast. Some have been sealed off by clay brought in by the last Ice Age and have thus become pools, best exemplified on Gower by Broad Pool beside the Cillibion - Reynoldston Road.

Great Tor, Tor Bay

47

Llanmorlais - Three Crosses 10

An easy walk to end with, mainly over fields and along quiet country lanes. Panoramic views over the Burry Estuary.

Distance: 8 miles (12.8 km)

The route starts at Llanmorlais Village in Station Road, just off the main road at GR 529947. There is a small car park, and buses pass here.

Walk east along Station Road and take the first footpath on the left, a wide stony track next to number 5. Very soon the bed of a dismantled railway is met, with a stile in the hedge. Do not go over the stile but turn left along the old railway for about 1/4 mile (0.4 km) to a footpath going along half right, signposted Mount Hermon, whose disused chapel can be seen on the skyline.

The path crosses two fields to the chapel and goes through the cemetery and out to a minor road. Cross the road to a car park with a stile on the right. Go over this and aim for another stile ahead on the skyline. Here, the Iron Age earthwork of Pen y Gaer is crossed half left, after which the left hand hedge is followed down to a stile and gate set back in the corner of the field.

Cross the stile and continue ahead on a track to meet a minor road. Turn right here for a short distance and take the first footpath on the left. Where this path begins to descend steeply with steps, go over the fence on the right, and take the path uphill to a seat with another path coming in on the right. This is a good place to pause and admire the view.

Carry on along the path which soon descends to meet a minor road, which is crossed to continue on a metalled lane. Shortly where the lane curves left go straight ahead across a small piece of rough ground, through a row of posts, just after which a path goes left through a gap in railings. Turn immediately right along a narrow surfaced path between houses. When a road is met, cross over to a small close of bungalows, bear right to go alongside No. 7 (Burry Heights) and walk between fencing panels along a twisting path to its end. Here, go right, over a stile, through the grounds of a house and, passing right of the house, out onto a road by Nant y Felin, site of the 17th Century Meyricks Mill.

10 Turn right, along the road past the old farm buildings of Parc Hendy, and when it swings right go straight on along a track and through a kissing gate to a path beside a stream. When the path meets a farm track keep right of it and cross the stream by a footbridge. Go uphill to another kissing gate and join a metalled lane, below the Blue Anchor public house. Turn left along this quiet lane, bright with wild flowers in spring and summer, passing Blaen Cedi, Heol Las and Tir Cethin farms. Above Tir Cethin, the estuary comes into view again. Keep on this lane to a T junction with a wider road. Turn right and stay on the road for a little over ½ mile (0.8 km)to the village of Three Crosses. (Note the Poundffald public house with the curved pound wall incorporated in the building).

Continue along the road and, when it swings left, keep straight on through the village and out onto Fairwood Common, over a cattle grid. Now take the first right, just after a copse, through a wide gateway and go along the track towards Gellihir Farm. Follow the waymarked footpath to the other side of Gellihir Farm.

The track crosses a small stream, then goes slightly right, up to a gate into a field (The wood on your left is a GWT nature reserve and may be entered by a stile on the left before the gate). Turn left and follow the hedge to a stile and cross to another field. Go along the right hand hedge to the next two stiles, emerging onto open common.

Continue in the same direction, with the field boundaries on your left, past a cottage, until joining a road by a small disused chapel (Carmel). Walk along the road to a junction, with a bungalow on the right. Just past the bungalow turn right, over a stile beside the entrance to Cerrig Man Farm. Walk along the field hedge parallel to the farm road until in the second field, go right, over a stile onto the road, then left and on to the farm. Go straight through the farm and continue on the road through pleasant wooded farmland. Shortly after crossing a small stream the way goes gently uphill and soon a stile is reached on the right. Go into the field, bearing left and crossing two further stiles to enter the churchyard of St. Illtyds, Llanyrnewydd. Turn left and leave by a kissing gate. Ahead is a housing estate.

Follow the road straight ahead into the housing estate. Turn left at the first junction and follow the road past houses until it becomes a lane. Continue along the lane to a road junction on a sharp bend. Turn left onto the road at the bend and continue along the road passing Cefn Bychan Farm down on the left. Bear right and, in about ¾ mile (1.25km), return to Hermon Chapel (opposite a small car park, visited earlier on this walk).

Go left through the cemetery again, but this time, take the stile on the left, just before the kissing gate. Follow the right hand hedge straight on to the next stile, and from here continue in the same direction, with trees on your right, to a pond with another stile alongside. The way now carries on along a low embankment, and after leaving the trees, swings left to the last stile in the corner of the field. You are now on the dismantled railway again and, in a few minutes, back to the start of the walk.

Yellowhammer

Castles

AFTER the Battle of Hastings in 1066, the Normans gradually extended their rule westwards and Gower was conquered in about 1100, becoming a Norman Marcher Lordship. There was fierce Welsh resistance for many years after this and the Normans built several castles in Gower to defend their territory. The first of these were mostly simple earth mound ringworks with wooden walls, towers and doors. But, later, stone castles were built and it is the remains of these that can be seen today.

Oystermouth was built in the late 13th Century and was the principal residence of the de Breos family, the Lords of Gower at that time. By the middle of the 14th Century its importance had diminished as Swansea Castle became the centre of power. It was "in ruins" by 1539, though part was still used as a court house and prison until 1650. It was later used as a quarry for stone, a squatters home and a cattle byre. It is now a picturesque tourist attraction and is the setting for a "Son et Lumiere" show at the Ostreme Festival held in August.

Pennard was probably built in the late 13th Century to replace a wooden one on the cliff on the other side of Pennard Pill. Legend tells that a chieftain warrior of Pennard Castle was disturbed at his wedding feast by fairy music and attempted to kill the fairy elves. Naturally, this was impossible and a voice sounded: "Poor chief! Thou warrest against those that shall now destroy thee. Thou has wantonly spoiled our innocent sport and for that thy castle and township shall be no more." The fairies vanished and clouds of sand came with whirlwind speed and overwhelmed everything. In fact, a succession of gales in the 14th and 15th Centuries gradually besanded the area of the castle and it was abandoned.

Penrice Park is probably one of the earliest enclosures in Gower and surrounds the largest and most impressive old castle in Gower. The keep, the oldest part of the castle, was probably built about 1240 by Robert de Penrice on the end of a limestone promontory. According to legend, the site is named after Rhys ap Caradog ap Iestyn, a Welsh leader who was captured and beheaded on this spot by the Normans in 1099 (Pen Rhys = head of Rhys).

About 100 years later, the walls were constructed, with the main gateway, its flanking towers and strongest defences on the north, where the castle was unprotected by cliffs or steep ground. By this time the Mansels were the Lords of the Manor and they gradually acquired most of South Gower and large areas of North Gower. In the 15th Century the large dovecote was added and held about 500 pigeons. They were eaten in the winter as a change from salted meat; the introduction of mangel-wurzels and winter feeding of cattle in the middle of the 19th Century meant cattle no longer had to be killed and salted down for the winter. This castle is on private land and cannot be visited.

By 1750, the Mansel family had no male heirs and the estate passed to the Talbots. The second of these, Thomas Mansel Talbot, inherited the property in 1758, and after a classical tour of the continent, became fired with enthusiasm for Italian art and architecture. As a result of this he commissioned the architect Anthony Keck to build a classical mansion just below the old castle, to house the works of art he had collected abroad. Work began in 1773, the ground was levelled and the road from Oxwich Bay improved to allow horses to haul materials brought by sea to the site, eg, bricks from Bridgewater, Bath stone from Bristol, slate from Lancaster, glass from London, paint from Gloucester and alabaster (gypsum) from Penarth. By 1779 the new mansion was completed. The grounds were landscaped and small ornamental lakes made by damming the stream from Millwood. T M Talbot was a founder member of the Glamorgan Agricultural Society and did much to improve the general estate management. He won an award for his reclamation scheme of a large area of Oxwich Marsh. The Towers, a folly castle serving as an entry lodge, at the NE corner of the estate on the A4118 - Oxwich road junction, was also built at this time.

The site of **Oxwich** castle has a long history of occupation and appears to have originally been a British hill fort on which a castle was later built by the Normans. Sir Rice Mansel was born in this Norman castle in 1487 and, after he had inherited the Penrice and Oxwich family estates, he built the present castle - really a fortified manor house - in the early part of the 16th Century on the same site. The impressive gateway, with the crest of the Mansel family above, is opposite the main block of the castle with its huge, first-floor hall. The ruined dovecote, similar to that at Penrice, clearly shows the nesting holes for the pigeons. The castle was abandoned by Sir Rice Mansel as his principal residence by the mid-1520s but continued to be occupied by Mansels. A "farmhouse" block was built on the south side shortly after.

In 1557, a fatal affray occurred as a result of the looting of a wrecked ship in Oxwich Bay by the Mansels and the local villagers. Sir George Herbert of Swansea marched with a body of armed men to Oxwich to reclaim what he considered his own. Lady Anne Mansel, an elderly lady, attempted to calm the resulting fracas outside the castle gate but was unfortunately struck on the head and severely injured by a stone thrown by one of Herbert's supporters. A cry of "murder!" went up and the antagonists were immediately sobered. Lady Anne died shortly afterwards and a later Star Chamber court hearing fined Sir George heavily, forced him to return the loot and to repair the damage he had caused. The outcome of the trial for Anne's death is not known. Conservation work on the castle has now been completed by Cadw and it can be visited. There is a small exhibition to be seen.

Weobley is a fortified manor house built in the late 13th-early 14th Century at the top of a 150-foot fossil sea cliff. These cliffs are now four miles from the sea at low tide, due to changing sea levels. The square tower to the right of the gatehouse is probably the oldest surviving part of the structure. The castle is thought to have been occupied by the de la Bere family up to the early 15th Century, when it was attacked and damaged in the Owain Glyndwr revolt. After this, it passed to Sir Rhys ap Thomas of Dynevor, who rebuilt and altered it extensively. By the mid

17th Century it was partly used as a farmhouse and belonged to the powerful Mansel family of Margam. Finally, it was put in the care of the Ministry of Works in 1911 (later Cadw) and can also be visited. There is a small exhibition here too.

One more stone castle remains to be mentioned: Bovehill, Landimore, another fortified manor house, dates from the 15th Century and was built by Sir Hugh Johnys, a Crusader Knight. His brass can be seen in St Mary's Church, Swansea. The scant remains are on private land and are not open to the public.

Oystermouth Castle

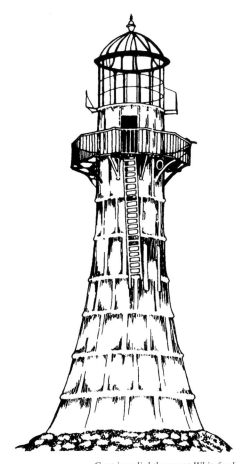

Cast-iron lighthouse at Whiteford